I0752968

what becomes of a body

a lyric progression

what becomes of a body

a lyric progression

kristina moriconi

Minerva Rising Press
Glen Ellyn

ISBN 978-1-950811-25-0

Cover Design: Maralynn Jacoby, Bear Left Bear
image: papaver rhoeas, from "Cyanotypes," Anna Atkins and Anne Dixon, public domain

Printed and bound in USA
First Printing April 2026

Published by Minerva Rising Press
864 Western Avenue
Glen Ellyn, IL 60137
www.minervarising.com

for my parents, who did the very best they could—
you will live forever in my heart

this body
is home, my childhood
is buried here, my sleep
rises and sets inside,
desire
crested and wore itself thin—
I live here.

—Lisel Mueller

Girl-child, breach-birth, limbs having petaled out too soon.

A mother broken open. A garden excavated and, from the wreckage
of our first day, our roots turned, all tuberous and tangled.

That night, the moon waning, though in its last-quarter phase,
the almanac having warned to avoid planting at all.

Yet here I am, baby-girl, unnamed perennial bloom.

And there we are, daughter-mother, a galaxy between us.
Our love position-dependent, grounded year after year in the need
to understand threshold and limitation.

I learn not to reach for her. Arms extended take up too much space.

I learn to be quiet, speak in apologies.

I learn to interpret maladies, how to correctly pronounce each one.

Everything from that earlier life tinged yellow with nicotine. Ashtrays overwhelmed.

Every surface polished with lemon Pledge.

Everything kept in its exact place. A museum of objects, collected, arranged in groups of three. Pineapples, artichoke finials, hip-knobs. Hummel figurines: one angel, one goose-girl, one boy in an apple tree.

My childhood bedroom, a realm into which I'd eventually retreat. There, my Madame Alexander fancy-dolls lined up perfectly right in front of me. A rapt audience assembled on bookshelves—their complicated dresses and hair and velvet ribbons I am not allowed to touch.

Until I do, little by little, deliberately changing something on one doll or another, as if daring myself to get caught.

A game, perhaps.

Dinner time, too. How I'll keep circling back to this story, over and over again.

I am not *hungry*, I say. *I'd rather starve,* words lassoed inside the thought-bubble of that defiant young girl I used to be.

For hours, I will myself to sit there at the round table in the round room without eating what's been heaped in front of me.

"You don't leave the table until you *make a sunshine.*" This, my parents' twisted phrase for the idea of how light will sparkle across the surface of an empty round plate.

I learn to dread dinner time. To quiet the rumble in my stomach. To stare up from the round table at the round clock on the wall, to sit alone in the round room late into the night and look out the darkened window for the round moon.

I trace the edges of things around me, to know how it feels
for line to take shape. To be reminded: every form desires a name.

Porkchop. T-bone.

Knife. Fork. Spoon.

I trace the edges of things around me so that I can feel safe.

My silence, as dissenting voice.

Time lapsed, wave-like.

Waiting—waiting——waiting———building————building———building.

Cresting-crash.

My mother often seems fragile. "She's not well today," my father says when I first start spending Saturdays with him, to give my mother *her time*.

He decides we will catch butterflies in a wooded area near our house, paths cut through dense thicket and bramble, spicebush and meadowsweet, fringes of honeysuckle.

He teaches me the sweeping method: *Slice the net through the air, smack it on the ground. Collect the butterfly into the back of the net.*

Trap it.

I try hard, but the idea of it—the harm—troubles me.

The more I do it, though—slice and smack, slice and smack—the easier it gets.

Before long, I am catching more than my father. Orange and black and yellow wings flutter madly in my net.

He opens his knapsack, pulls out glass jars he's brought along. He offers one to me. I twist off the lid, smell the alcohol inside, feel it sting my nose—cotton soaked in my father's gin lines the bottom of each jar.

I stand at his side, silent, watch as he gathers up the mesh of his net, gives the butterfly no choice but to flap frantically through the glass mouth of *the killing jar*.

Its ghastly fate.

One by one, the flap of wings slows, stops.

By the time we make it back to my father's workbench, our specimens are relaxed, pliable.

His instructions, part of a strange new vocabulary.

They're delicate. Especially the scales, they rub off easily.

As I do as he says, my hands tremble. As I *pinch* the thorax, *spread* the wings, *push* tiny insect pins to hold each specimen in place.

Though I think it a thousand times, I never bring myself to confess: *I don't want to do this.*

It will risk disappointing him, I know, his face beaming with pride.

I learn: Silence can protect. And it can endanger.

Sometimes, it unburdens.

Sometimes, it becomes unbearable.

I learn: Stored properly, specimens last for years.

And the stillness, the lack of movement, it stays with me.

The sound: slice <smack> slice <smack> slice <smack>

How a body can become liability.

How this in-between time in my life brings with it a want to make smaller what I see as burdensome. To flatten emerging curves, become less visible.

Less desirable.

This, perhaps, its own kind of freedom.

To create the illusion. To suggest.

Misdirection. Attention drawn to one thing to distract from another.

Something appears. Something disappears.

Something defies gravity.

At sixteen, I try hard to get the needle on the scale to flutter below 100, to rest finally at 99 pounds.

Ribs, countable. Convex. Arcing into a series of parentheses on either side. Body as incidental, slipped in between.

I want my mother to notice, to cross the unseeable line, come for me.

She does not.

This will be its own kind of loss.

Mother-daughter, a problem of math. Balance, perhaps. Order of operations.

Subtraction. My want for less-than, physically.

Addition. My need for control, greater-than. How that becomes what I believe protects me, what I cannot live without.

When I faint during a school assembly, a teacher steps in, offers counsel.

He gains my trust.

And I share with him the little notebook I've been keeping, a daily chronicling of food consumed, an accounting of calories.

Sometimes, a day's page might read: *1 apple, 95.*

At first, we meet in his classroom after school. I confide in him. I reveal my conflicts, my struggle with self-confidence. I mention my parents, as much as I can understand, speak of how it is they seem to have withdrawn, become unreachable.

All of this is normal for a woman my age, he assures me. It's the classic struggle for independence.

"And the not eating, that's your way of thinking you can control what is happening in your world." He looks at me, waves his hand in the air as if holding a wand. "You believe you can make those numbers on the scale fall, like magic." He flicks his wrist. "Poof! Disappearing act as act of defiance."

It all makes sense.

Until it doesn't. Until words become just a series of sounds and sound drowns out whatever once seemed certain. Or solid. Or safe.

Through the open window of the classroom, I hear children playing on the playground across the street. Laughing. Shouting.

I hear the bounce of a ball on concrete.

thump <ring> thump <ring> thump <ring> thump <ring>

What happens inside that classroom makes no sound.

With the exception, perhaps, of a screech, a desk's metal feet sliding across the linoleum floor. Though I will only recall my startle at its abrupt movement.

How it is one place, then another.

How I am one place, then another.

How his hands are one place, then another.

I learn: To give sound to that immediate space will mean I'll have to inhabit that body again.

That body. Sixteen. Blue uniform skirt hung on sharp-angled hip bones. White blouse tucked, buttoned over clavicle and ribs, protruding and countable.

Through the open window of the classroom, I hear children playing on the playground across the street. Laughing. Shouting.

I hear the bounce of a ball on concrete.

thump <ring> thump <ring> thump <ring>

It will take years for me to understand why the sound of kids playing on the playground will gut me whenever I hear it again.

thump <ring> thump <ring>

That sound will remind me of loss.

thump <ring>

Of something taken from me.

That day.

The clock on the wall beats. My heart ticks.

Fight-or-flight, sympathetic nerves triggered—everything, for-the-rest-of-my-life, unsafe, impending catastrophe.

I learn: The brain couples sound with emotional information,
bundles and stores it, even if we want to forget.

The amygdala in the front of the brain links fear with sound memory.
thump <ring> thump <ring>

Waves of air drift, reach the eardrum, brush against its small bones,
shivering through them like wind through trees.

I consider, too, how the intensity of sound is measured in decibels (dB).

How near total silence registers at 0 dB & a whisper at 15 dB. And a normal conversation at 60 dB. And the loudest (verified) human scream at 129 dB.

I hang on, as what-happened-to-me falls somewhere deep into the explanatory gap.

Qualia collect, stack up—deep-down, ineffable. Nowhere can I locate the language I need, in this instance, in this body, to say: *this, this is what it's like to be—*

Who would listen anyway?

Protection is a myth.

The teacher will never be found out. Or maybe he will. And in-secret, without a sound, he'll be moved to another school.

Either way, it is too late.

For me.

For every girl like me.

Wherever he lands.

To hide, a flower mantis relies on a form of camouflage, aggressive mimicry.

To avoid being identified.

Skin, semi-crystalline. Limbs, bent, ready to seize its prey.

In response to distress, the body's sympathetic nervous system activates, triggers a cascade of reactions.

Freeze— Flight— Fight— [the uproar]

Fright— Flag— Faint— [the shutdown]

Fear. Astonishment. How both lead to the senses of sight and hearing being instantly aroused. Eyes open wide, eyebrows raised.

The skin pale. Breath accelerated, shallow. The mouth dry.

That summer, our backyard is overrun by Japanese beetles, metallic green with copper wings. They chew through every leaf, sparing only its network of lacelike veins. My father's gardens fill with fragile skeletons of foliage that had once thrived.

He wages a battle when they come for his marigolds. He sprays, sets traps. He mumbles obscenities.

That summer, I say few words.

That summer, a continuum of waiting—for the-what-will-happen—
for the-dreaded-eventual—for the-next.

I obsess that summer over Sylvia Plath's hyphens when I read her poems for the first time.

Compounding.

A linguistic unit composed of elements able to be understood both independently as well as when coupled.

Wholly-new words formed by Plath's compounds bear figurative meaning.

Each baring metaphor.

eye-stones, fen-frost, moon-eye, wedding-cake face

snake-warp, snake-weft, dark-suited, thin-paned

Time-hinged, slams open.

And, in the-going-forward, there exists no-unknowing.

Fastened together, fixed points of juncture persist. Place as fact, rather than feeling. Rid of impression.

A pattern of moments, occasions: predatory—invasive. A tending toward harm.

Fear-memories cast shadows in the brain, become permanent forms.

Misophonia is a condition—or disorder, or syndrome—in which common sounds can trigger reactivity.

The average duration of symptoms is twenty-one years, though that number increases if repetitive exposure to misophonic triggers continues.

What happens next happens in the shadow of the same high school building: the high school building that housed the classroom: the same classroom that held the desk: the desk with metal feet: the same metal feet that may or may not have screeched across the linoleum floor.

What if a surface holds onto each disturbance brought to it, layered upon it?

The parking lot, an ordinary school night: A man—a-stranger-pretending-to-be-an-impatient-parent—asks for the time—

The time is 7:05 when he grabs my friend.

7:05 when he pushes her up against a car.

7:05 when he lifts a knife from his pocket, presses its thin edge to her neck. Skin, resisting.

I stand there, six or seven feet away, consider the scissors inside my backpack. Consider where on a body one might be able to plunge them deepest, where there might be the least obstruction from muscle, bone.

I begin to back away slowly.

My friend cries. He is on top of her.

Everything reduces to shape.

I turn.

Run.

And his words cut through everything:

IfyourunI'llkillher.

And I trip down some stairs.

And I pull open the red door. The scrape of metal against metal, the shudder-slam of its closing behind me.

And I scream into the building:

He. *Is.* *Raping.* *Her.*

And yellow tape is draped around the periphery.

And a police officer drives me and my friend to the station.

And our mothers (not fathers) arrive, sit alongside each of us in small glass rooms, where we're asked, separately, to tell—to retell—our story.

Where we're asked to select eyes and nose and mouth from a flip-book of features, to build—rebuild—the face of a monster.

I feel the burn of acid in my throat. I feel the metal chair cold against the bare skin of my legs.

My mother does not touch me or console me. As though in keeping her distance she can somehow deny this dreadful reality. Her body stiffened, matchstick-struck, already setting fire to every word of this.

Ash, swept.

Hush.

Tongue-held.

Somewhere I read: what is feared most by humans are encounters with coyotes and mountain lions. Aliens are a close third.

I fear men.

In my first year of college, I learn to purge.

Locked in the bathroom, I kneel on the fluffy pink rug, puke until my throat burns. I can't bring myself to binge first, as I assume is the proper way, so the process can be a struggle. Long. Laborious.

Sometimes I am loud. Sometimes unsteady, afterward.

No one seems to notice.

I spend a lot of time inside my head wanting to be an artist, suspended somewhere between my pragmatic, conventional upbringing and my desire to create passionately, without reticence. Without the kind of strict control I'd assimilated.

Graphic design as a major seems to straddle the two. Creating, but within the boundaries of a somewhat structured set of rules.

I study principles. Theories.

Of alignment, contrast, repetition.

Of tension, balance, symmetry.

First-year figure drawing is a requirement. Nude models. For weeks before, I anticipate the experience. Think: awkward. Think: embarrassing.

The classroom an arc of easels and stools set around an improvised platform. A place at the center where a model sits or stands. Or reclines.

On the first day, newsprint pads flipped open, propped upright, brand-new pieces of charcoal pressed to the blank page, a man walks into the room, throws his robe onto a chair, sits down and rests both his hands on his knees.

The first time I see a body completely naked, other than my own.

There is a moment initially when I want to turn away, to avert my eyes. In staying focused, though, my perception shifts. The body—the folds and creases of its skin, become like those of fabric, those of leaf and flower. All light and shadow. Contour and shading.

The marks I make are subtle, faint. Uncertain.

The teacher insists on bold lines, orbits the room gesturing wildly, as if to render a figure in the air. As though to draw out from each of us this kind of passion, this boundless energy. Untamed.

At first, I resist.

Then, slowly, I let my hand slacken, my arm sweep wider, losing the burden of expectation, accuracy.

And in bold, looser lines, I sculpt a kind of darkness on the page.

It feels unfamiliar.

. . .

On a crumpled sheet, I unmake my own body.

Shadow, smudged.

I study typography, too. Letterform as part of typeface, typeface as component of font.

There is a whole new language I acquire: Baseline, cap-height, x-height, ascender, descender. Serif, sans serif.

Crossbar, stem, shoulder, arm, leg, tail. Counter, bowl.

Kerning, leading, tracking.

I am comforted by the exactness of this discipline, the elements of hierarchy and consistency that apply. A pattern of the golden ratio to abide by. Balance to consider, white space to utilize.

This, the kind of artistic pursuit perhaps even my parents can get behind. Practical. Focused. Potentially income-producing.

From a densely wooded area on campus, the deafening sound of cicadas draws me in.

As I walk along a trampled path, I see hundreds of abandoned brown shells clinging to trunks of trees.

I decide to collect them, paint them white, create my first art installation by returning them, ghostlike, to the woods, arranged in linear and circular and radiating patterns for others to find.

I tell no one about this, though, too worried, too uncertain.

How might such an oddity be seen?

Kiki Smith comes to mind, her imagining, her rendering of the unexpected, her compulsive need to make things, to gather together disparate items, to investigate possible new meanings that can surface when things are assembled and juxtaposed.

Exuviae, I call my impromptu exhibit. It is the name for those shells split open, shed as part of the cicada's life cycle.

There is so much that happens, so much left unnoticed—the repetition, the necessary sequence of things, what sometimes gets left behind. With Exuviae, I want to remind people of that, by re-constructing—in situ—for the cicada, a kind of in-memory.

The soundtrack for my installation begins each day in the evening around dusk. The noise, a kind of beautiful distraction, in real-time. The buckling and unbuckling of the cicada's ribs, tymbals. Clicks hastening, becoming a high-pitched buzzing sound. Like the sharp edge of scissors pressed to a grind wheel.

My on-campus job brings hours of silence, days alone archiving books in the windowless basement of the library. I feel at home there, navigating the warren of its rooms. Across thresholds, alongside thousands of volumes strangely familiar, I find a cadence, move through the cave-like space as though its map had long-before been etched on my mind.

There, I slip old books out from protective cellophane, pluck signature cards from folders inside cover-boards. On each, a story—signatures, stamped-dates.

Within the turn of these pages, all of these people had journeyed, in some way, each having been transformed.

This matters to me, this ephemera of the book.

This preservation.

At the start of June, just after my second year of college ends, I go to the local bank, think I recognize the boy behind the counter, the one who signals for me to come to his window.

Maybe I've seen him on campus.

He wears a pinstriped shirt, its collar buttoned on either side of a red paisley tie. When he looks at me, his whole face smiles, a small dimple notching one cheek.

I return his smile, blushing.

"I've seen you on campus." He smiles again. "You an art major?"

"Graphic design. How about you?"

"Double-major, Business and Finance. I'm hoping to manage a bank someday."

"Well, you look the part already," I say, thinking how my face must've been as red as his tie.

I am practiced neither at flirting nor recalling conversations. But these moments seem to insist on mattering, being remembered. How the words, the gestures, even the light that day, all seems to sculpt itself into memory.

As he slides a receipt back to me, I write my phone number on the back of one his business cards. "It's my parents' house number. I'm not around much, so leave a message with my mother. Or on the machine." He takes the card, hands me a lollipop. When I turn to leave, I look back, see him smiling still.

He calls, same day.

I'm smitten.

And I trip-up trying to navigate the space between us.

Trust—as either noun or verb—is neither a thing nor an action I understand. For me, it seems volatile. I feel too visible, at-risk.

Epinephrine floods the bloodstream, circulates, revs the body's physiological state.

With harm (sustained in the absence of voice/requisite vocabulary) comes heightened vigilance.

How to make space for another when *alone* has been my synonym for *safe*.

I keep trying to slow my pulse, to loosen the knots that tighten in my shoulders. To let go.

Our first date, a movie.

Our next date—a picnic—a blanket in the park.

On our third date, he takes me to the elementary school he'd long-ago attended in the city. We play basketball in the schoolyard. P-I-G. And I am convinced he lets me win. In a local dive-bar nearby, we watch the Celtics play. He knows every player, every statistic. He screams at the television screen.

Afterward, in the backseat of his car, we steam up windows, undress slowly.

My body resists, at first, pulls away. But he is sweet, unhurried, without me having to say anything.

For the first time, another body drawn-close feels safe. I am steadied. I am seen, held, and I don't want to run away.

Not sure why, but that summer we keep each other secret, except for the women he works with at the bank.

Most of our dates involve a picnic blanket. Or a parked car, a vacant lot sheltered by trees, a dark street.

Eventually, when he says *I love you,* I say it back.

That same summer, I spend my days working in an art store, fixed still on wanting to be an artist.

And, religiously, I take my body on long runs.

On the day of a work-party I'm invited to, I wake to go for a run first, a few miles around the neighborhood with my Walkman. I've made a mixtape of songs I think match my running pace.

The beat of the music urges me along, a distance much farther than I plan to go. But it feels good.

Around midday, I start to make the brownies I'd promised to bring to the party.

A box-mix, though what I need to add depends entirely on whether I want *fudgy* brownies or *cake-like* brownies.

Sometimes: the smallest decisions.

I go with cake-like: 3 eggs, ¼ cup water, ½ cup oil. I follow the directions, each step: Preheat the oven to 350 degrees, grease the bottom of the glass pan. Mix the eggs, water, and oil in a large bowl, add in the brownie mix, stir until well-blended.

I pour the mixture into the pan, slide it onto the center rack in the oven, set the timer for 27 minutes.

I keep looking through the oven window. Watching. Waiting.

But, oddly, the mixture doesn't bake; it stays more liquid than solid. I return to the directions on the box, thinking perhaps there's something I've done wrong.

And there is: instead of ¼ cup of water, I'd added ¾ cup.

Sometimes: the smallest mistakes.

I drive to get another box-mix.

On my second attempt, I pay closer attention, and they turn out perfect,
a shiny, crinkly thin crust on top, a slightly darker crust along the edge.
My previous error, though, has caused me to run late.

I leave the house in a hurry, wondering, after a few minutes, if I remembered to say goodbye to my parents. I think about turning around, but I'm already late.

Sometimes: the smallest consideration.

As I round a curve, I switch on my windshield wipers, rain falling lightly.

What happens next is a blur of something big and metal, spinning. Rushing toward me.

Total darkness, alone. I feel nothing, like my body isn't there.

My teeth swim inside my mouth, and I try to keep them beneath my tongue.

I hear someone yelling, someone pounding on the window.

Sirens grow louder.

Sound becomes the way I take in what is happening around me.

screech <thrum> screech <thrum>

Someone takes hold of my right hand. I hear a woman on the passenger side of the car, her voice soft and slow, and I try to listen.

clang <snap> clang <snap>

I blink the faces of strangers in the window beside me.

I know I should be feeling pain somewhere—anywhere—everywhere—in my body.

Yet, nothing.

.   .   .

I see words, serifed and soaring: *Stay.*   *Here.*

I see a blackbird pray.

With the driver-side door finally pried open, a firefighter leans in, speaks to me, his words sifted through a strange filter. Muffled. Making only half-sense.

"We may have to amputate your left leg, but I am trying not to…"

From behind him—or beside him—another man shouts, "The firewall's cracked. This thing's gonna blow."

The firefighter does not leave my side.

The loud rip of a saw through metal drowns out the drone of voices, becomes almost soothing to me. I forget about my leg, about the teeth I hold under my tongue.

I think about my parents, wonder what they are doing right now.

As the firefighter struggles to stabilize my neck, I glimpse my face in the dangling rearview mirror, see bright-red pooled where my mouth used to be.

clang <snap> clang <snap> clang <snap>

screech <thrum> screech <thrum> screech <thrum>

The roof of the car is saw-cut, lifted away. A loud rev of engines commences, and I feel some kind of force tug at my body—forward—backward.

"Stop!" The firefighter screams. He leans in. "Are you okay?"

I am not okay. Nothing is okay.

I start to think this might be a dream. And I will wake up soon, walk down the hallway of my parents' house, go out to my car, drive to my friend's party with my perfect brownies.

screech <thrum> screech <thrum> screech <thrum> screech <thrum>

My body is strapped to a board, hoisted, somehow separated from the car, my head positioned so that I cannot move it at all. Split-second, the sky.

.   .   .

I begin speaking to the bluest butterfly.

Listen. Its rhapsodic reply, like poem.   Elegy.

Siren again, the sensation of hurtling forward, how it frightens me.

Much later, I will learn that every second of that drive had fallen somewhere in the infinitesimal space between my life's continuance and its end.

I try to focus on the cadenced hum of voices. Bodies surrounding me.

Cocooned.

The loud backup beep of the ambulance in the hospital parking lot. An immediate volley of medical language. For the third or fourth time, I hear: "female, nineteen years of age…car accident…internal bleeding…possible neck fracture." And something about my heart I cannot understand.

The bed beneath me arcs through the air.

The sound of my parents' voices, muffled.

"Trauma, level one," someone yells, over and over.

A pool of blood in the shape of a girl, I am wheeled into a cold room, white ceilings, fluorescent light. A nurse suctions my mouth and throat. She talks to me, slowly, tells me what she is doing, keeps apologizing as I gag.

Then a gloved hand comes toward my face from the other side of the bed, snaps the bones of my nose back into place. Still, I do not feel pain, only the sensation of energy transferred—this applied force, the sound of suction and bone cracking in this too-bright place—the last thing I'll remember.

.   .   .

Wing after wing, into the darkness.

All the injured songbirds in shoeboxes.

Existing everywhere and nowhere.   Displaced.

When I wake, it is to the sound of a soft voice singing, accompanied by a steady beep, an alternating hiss and click.

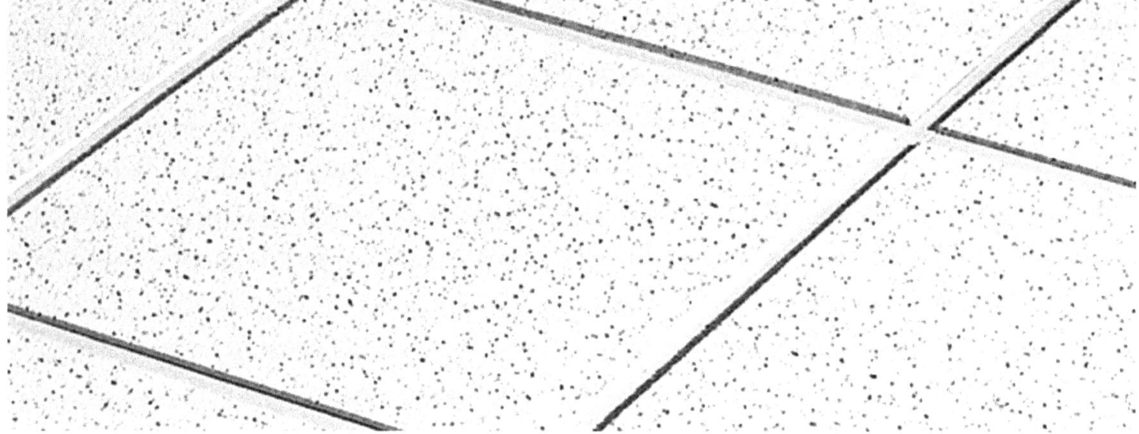

Visually, my world has been reduced to a landscape of ceiling tiles directly above my bed.

If I roll my eyes to the right, I see part of a machine, a glass wall behind it. To the left, something on that side of my face obstructs my sight peripherally.

My thoughts lift, paper-lantern-like. And, at some point, my body drifts up toward them, hovers there, long enough to glimpse the girl in the bed below: tubes and wires tethering her to multiple machines, her left leg braced, elevated in a kind of sling, her face covered in gauze bandages. So much bright white, almost blinding.

I slip in and out of sleep, learn slowly to navigate this new world. To listen for footfalls, to notice the shift of light and shadow across the room as hours pass, as day lapses into night.

In the confines of a hospital bed, its rails, my body is turned from one side to another. I cannot will the right side of my body to move, no matter how hard I try.

Eventually, I am taken back to the operating room.

This pattern forms, back and forth, the only way I leave the small glass space I've come to occupy.

Still I cannot walk.

I cannot talk.

.   .   .

I stumble upon a field of daisies, plead with a hummingbird to lend me its wings—

beyond this,

                                        a magnolia tree—

hours spent swimming in its teacup blooms, pollen-drunk.

Stowed-away.

The story of that day, its subsequent days, is dispensed to me in small, fractured pieces.

I learn my mother had been in the kitchen making dinner, my father in his backyard garden picking tomatoes, when two police officers had knocked on the front door.

They both dropped everything, followed the police car, sirens blasting all the way to the hospital. And they arrived at the trauma center early, at least an hour before I'd been rolled past them.

And they'd heard everything the EMTs communicated to the nurses during the two hours it had taken to free me from the crumpled metal of my car.

.   .   .

On the verge between meadow and forest, swallowtails lured by brambles.

The arc and twist of split-stems weave themselves into days—

weeks—

fractured mandibular alveolus

4 displaced teeth: #23, #24, #25, #26

metal arch bar fixed in place with wire

laceration, left lateral border, approx. 1.0 in.

laceration, mandible, center, approx. .5 in.

laceration, mandible, left vertical, approx. 1.25 in.

C5 spinal cord injury—fused/ nerves decompressed

3 lower rib fractures, flail chest

splenetic rupture (grade V)—splenectomy

liver laceration (>75% of hepatic lobe)—sutured

insertion of closed suction drain (lower abdomen)

muscle and ligament tear, dislocated shoulder joint

Bennett fracture, involving carpometacarpal joint

vertical inline incision, median sternotomy

closed with sutures, staples, stainless steel wire

multiple blood transfusions (type A positive)

tibial shaft open fracture, proximal

dashboard removal (knee)

medial patellofemoral ligament reconstruction

ankle joint, nondisplaced fracture

My body, its restoration, is documented in an ongoing series of photographs. The process of rephotography, a diachronic *then* and *now*. A careful study stored in a three-ring binder, each page accompanied by clinically accurate notations.

Body as encyclopedia, information presented in fragmentary forms. Reports. Tallies. Lists. Timelines.

When I can finally hold a pen, on the pages of a notebook, I begin to write things down, take accurate notes, sometimes, like a medical textbook page.

Or, more often, I record strange random details of my day—like the color of the Jell-O on my hospital tray, the names of the doctors who come by, the number of times I hear a trauma announcement made.

Note: Passage of time inside a hospital is not the same as it is outside.

Note: Time is measured by dosages, bags of fluid, diagnoses, vital signs.

Note: Progress looks like staples and stitches removed. Tubes and I.V. bags taken away.

Note: Progress sounds like less beeping, hissing, clicking, bells ringing. Less footsteps of doctors. Less bad news.

Perhaps, someday, I will need all of it to have mattered in some way.

I become intrigued by the idea of pieces—taken apart. The break. The brokenness. How perhaps the too-big can be made bearable.

Information parsed.

The notion of what existed—what exists—in between. Before. After.

How I will come to grasp the story of that day and every day since then.

How it assembles, bit by bit.

Sometimes, the wave of visitors in and out each evening overwhelms the room. I am thankful for the company, but it also reminds me:

> When I speak, it is harder to breathe.
>
> When I smile, I feel the tug of stitches in the corner of my mouth, across my cheek and chin.
>
> When I cough, I have to hold a pillow against my chest, press hard so it doesn't feel like my ribs are being cracked open again and again and again.

Sometimes people curve around the foot of my bed and, from where I sit—bound and propped—they seem like spectators. Onlookers. And I feel like a thing to be pitied.

Some just smile.

One brings me the newspaper she has saved from that day. As though I might want to keep it. A souvenir. A prize.

I am the tragedy.

> Photo. Headline. Caption.
>
> *Accident aftermath.*
>
> *Crash victim.*

Stuck somewhere between *Obituaries* and *Funeral Notices.*

Life and death, separated here on the newsprint page by a narrow column of letterforms, flush-left, Times Roman, 12-point.

And from this newspaper, I will learn: On that same day, an opera singer died in New York City, a ballerina in Paris. A British maverick. An international pistol champion. A crane operator. A basketball player.

Which is to say: we are all just seconds away.

Assumptions shattered.

Perception shifted. A need to reframe, to understand time in another way—perhaps as a kind of waiting room, both temporal and spatial.

Place as circumstance, rather than impression. Everything compressed to line, angle and curve.

How unsettling it had been in the car, in the ambulance, when I hadn't felt pain.

Now, pain fully inhabits my body.

And how small the space between threshold and tolerance.

I hold tight to the button that sends morphine reeling through my veins. Summer-fling-turned-love visits me every day, brings with him each time a single yellow rose. The nurses collect them into vases for me. The vases overflow the windowsill, spillover onto bedside tables.

Summer-fling-turned-love is there by my side the day the plastic surgeon arrives to remove the bandages from my face. The day before, I'd sworn to him I would never smile again.

I am scared. And he holds my hand.

And, one day, from his pocket, he presents me with a ring.
Black onyx, tiny diamonds on each side.

I smile, and the stitches in the corner of my mouth stretch.
Burn. Remind me.

What worries me most—what I try hardest to find words for—is the awareness, the knowing that I will never be the same again.

To resolve that this will be the only true thing I'll ever know.

For years, I will look for the right language to compile my jottings, as I call them at first. My inventory of scraps.

A catalogue, slow-built.

I turn twenty that summer, in my hospital room. The nurses throw a party for me, tie balloons to my I.V. pole, give me cards, buy me an extra-large milkshake.

A few days later, after the last tube is removed—a pump connected to my abdomen—I am told I'll be discharged.

Soon.

Tomorrow.

Early.

I know I should be happy about leaving the hospital, but I am more afraid than anything. Here, on the fourth floor of the Highland Building, there is a call-button. There are nurses, doctors who can be paged. There is a routine to each of my days.

It is safe.

I know once I cross the threshold of those automatic-doors downstairs, feel the fresh air on my face, I will have to get into a car again. I will have to return to my parents' house—indefinitely.

I will have to face who I am outside these walls. And who I am not anymore.

.   .   .

I see myself leave without me.

My body is rebuilt in stages. I schedule follow-up surgeries, look ahead at weeks—months—years—of mending.

When I'm honest with myself, alone, I'm angry a lot, and I cry.

More often, I lie, make it look as though I can handle anything. It's easy, actually. People see what they want to see.

In the silence of my parents' house, a history of words unspoken, emotions unfelt, I am expected to put everything behind me, let it go, move on. As though that day—and all the days after—had never happened at all.

Here, in the too-small house, silence becomes the star-cluster in which we live, orbiting one another without saying a word.

In their living room, I spend my days and nights in a hospital bed.

On the floral sofa across from me, my mother reads *Good Housekeeping, Better Homes & Gardens, Country Living.*

All around me, on shelves and on walls: Hummel figurines, Norman Rockwell plates. A small gathering of timeless, voiceless characters assembled in the quiet room.

Across the silence, I glimpse my mother now and then, from what seems miles away.

I remember trying to connect, one time sharing with her a dream I'd had—a revised version of the car accident, an adaptation, a narrative in which I die.

In that moment, I long to be lulled, to believe I am safe.

In that moment, my mother looks up, says to me, "I never dream."

I tell her that she does dream—everyone dreams—she just can't recall hers.

That is the end of the conversation. She returns to the embroidery hoop resting in her lap.

Out of nowhere, on a random weekday, I return from a physical therapy appointment to find ripped-out the dense rows of azalea bushes that had once bordered the backyard. Soil along the slight embankment loosened, some entwined ends of roots lopped-off, left behind.

My mother seems restless. Her ashtray always full.

My father works excessive hours.

When he decides to build a shed in the backyard, I finally get to see him.
I watch as he draws up plans for construction. He is patient. Precise.
He measures and saws, assembles wall frames.

I hold tight to his words. Suspended.

For the front wall double-door opening, he uses a load-bearing header to support the weight of the roof trusses.

This, we can talk about. Language again as instruction—slice and smack—words as means to an end.

I feel like I can't heal fast enough.

And driving—being in a car, even as a passenger—terrifies me.

My mind unstoppable. A series of seismic events.

A landslide.

Memory, the images it stores, a profusion of red, its near-constant intrusion.

The red of crumpled car-metal from which I'd been freed. The soaked-red of shoelaces. The red of a face trapped in a rearview mirror. The flashing-red of siren. The red of hemorrhage, where snapped ribs sent sharp-splintered ends through organs, the gloved hands of surgeons reaching in to stem the tide. Bagged blood hung, transfused through tubes, circulating inside my body.

Again and again, all of it summoned up.

Symptoms of post-traumatic stress disorder most commonly begin within three months of the traumatic event. But they sometimes emerge later.

Sometimes as depression. Sometimes as detachment, that sense of being an observer—outside—rather than a participant—inside—an experience.

And sometimes as re-experiencing. Reliving an event so vividly the heart gallops. The mind in pursuit, chasing dark shadows in dreams, in distressing thoughts.

Everything unresolvable.

Blame.

Anger.

Guilt.

Shame.

[silence]

Back on campus, me and summer-fling-turned-love stay a secret. He sneaks into my room sometimes. He is patient with me.

Physically. I cannot even kiss him.

Emotionally. Often, I cry in his arms.

Between restoring my body and hauling the remnants of it to classes every day, I am exhausted.

It all seems too much, the push and pull, the sudden swerve of my desire.
How I retreat, then days—weeks—later, I plead with him to come back.

He had known me, *before*. There is comfort in that knowing.

But that lighter, less-afraid version of me is gone. I miss her, and I believe he does, too.

Here, in this unbridled *after*, I have no idea how to grieve what is lost, no idea how to ask him for help in doing that.

Instead, a pattern forms, sustained for a while, spanning weeks first.
Then months.

My enthusiasm for nearly everything dwindles.

Dies.

The truth of what happened to me discouraged, untold. Tidied up, packed away.

Hundreds of notebook pages left blank.

I consider ripping them out, setting them side by side, their wild untrimmed spiral-edges tangling—another exhibit. Perhaps: *Everything Hushed.*

Over winter break that year, a follow-up surgery is scheduled, a scar-revision I'd been postponing for months.

My face, a topographic map, its natural and man-made features, contour lines drawn to trace the course of someone else's risk-taking.

Some else's mistake: to press the gas pedal instead of the brake, accelerate into a sharp curve, spinning on a road surface wet with rain—spinning—side-swiping—spinning—striking head-on.

I will never again look the same. No matter how many surgeries to revise the scars, still, they remain.

And I cannot recall how I looked *before*. Instead, images of that day flash over and over on the wall of an otherwise empty room, disorienting me.

A moth, drawn to a light—mistaken—spiraling to its doom.

During the procedure—twilight sedation—I wake somewhat, my eyes blinking open to the bright fluorescence, to the plastic surgeon's gloved fingers slowly drawing thread up, away from my face.

A strange sensation.

My body, a tapestry. My skin, fabric hand-spun.

Afterward, in the unsettling quiet of my parents' house, my face heals. Eating is impossible—no holiday cookies, no holiday dinner. I drink an occasional can of Ensure, for its necessary nutrients/calories, but mostly I watch as my body becomes less-than, once again.

While I do not want to let my eating-disordered voice back in, it lodges itself inside my head anyway, whispers: *You can lose ten pounds here without even trying. Remember, you're already the tragedy. Everyone already thinks: Poor-girl.*

By the time my last semester of college begins, I am featherlike, flitting from class to class, caffeinating myself sometimes to the point of hand tremors.

I take flight, circle fast, land unsteady on edges.

Razor-thin.

I stay awake nights in a row working on my senior thesis project. *Spin!* The voice inside my head insists. *Keep spinning!*

Days dull.

Nights sharpen.

In the middle of one brief deep-sleep, I wake thirsty. In the darkness I collide with a desk chair left not in its usual place. On its sharp corner, I smack my left knee.

It swells immediately, filling up with fluid.

The pain immediate. Intense.

I end up in the emergency room.

After spraying my knee with something to numb it, the doctor prepares a large syringe.

"Be thankful you're in here," he says. "The waiting room is packed with kids here with their friend. He was struck by lightning."

"Oh no." I blink open my eyes briefly. "I hope he's okay."

"No. He didn't make it," the doctor says, as the needle simultaneously punctures my skin.

I feel the pressure, deep inside my knee. I feel it burn.

My thoughts race.

I think about the boy.

About the unlikely odds of being struck by lightning.

I think about his friends, waiting.

The doctor stabilizes my knee, asks a nurse to bring crutches.

In motion slowed by uncertainty, by not-knowing, I watch as my classmates spill out from the waiting room, walk toward me.

I hear them ask why I'm here.

I hear them tell me that summer-fling-turned-love had been struck by lightning.

But he's fine, I hear someone say, with certainty.

In my head, the doctor's words repeat: *No. He didn't make it.*

No.

He didn't make it.

No.

He.

Didn't.

Make.

It.

My leg buckles.

I lean hard on the crutches, hold onto the impossibly heavy burden of this thought: All of them think he's still alive.

I long more than anything to unknow what I know: What none of them know yet.

None of them know that he's died.

None of them know that his skin blossomed with lightning flowers, Lichtenberg fractals branching in fern-leaf patterns.

Replicating across a body I'd once held in my arms.

In the same wooded area, on the same campus, among the same trees where in-secret I'd situated my ensemble of ghost cicadas, there would be a metal keg, a flash of blue-white light across an electric field.

Luminescent. Incandescent.

His heart would stop instantly.

In the unsettling quiet of my parents' house, my leg heals.

My heart empties, flings itself against the once-cleft bones of its cage.

Mostly, I remain unaware of things going on. The bedroom in my parents' house a kind of vault into which I close myself: shades pulled down, lights turned off, door locked. Rarely do I step beyond its threshold.

Mostly, I stop eating.

Stop showering.

Stop caring.

I can think only—obsessively—about what my last words to him had been. In every version of remembering, I sound angry.

The first time I leave the house, it is for the funeral.

It rains that day.

A sea of umbrellas rolls slowly toward the church.

My mother is there. She grips my forearm as we walk toward the casket.

I see the women he worked with at the bank, and they each hug me.

There will be newspaper headlines. An article written in which my mother is interviewed: "He was a great kid, never missed a day visiting my daughter when she was in the hospital..."

There will be a dedication ceremony for him on campus: a small rose garden with a plaque, a wooden bench beside it.

There will be graduation beneath a big tent in the middle of the soccer field. There will be a metal chair where he would've sat. A single yellow rose left on its seat.

Again, I don't leave the house.

I want my mother to come for me, but everything she had to say she'd said already in that newspaper interview.

All her words corralled, used up.

For days, weeks, afterward, she disappears into a sewing project. Each small, hand-cut, patchwork-piece hand-stitched into a patterned square.

The squares accumulate, each one pinned to another then hand-stitched into a larger assembly of squares. Fabric strips affixed between them, batting and backing and binding pressed, held together.

An act of addition. This way she meticulously measures each distance, structures her world.

I begin crafting my own connections.

What I find, unintentional at first.

And what is found, I assemble on the page.

At once a moment
gave way to
an "unforseeable curve" —
commencement
of history —
the intermingling of metal
an orchestra playing
at the edge —
a shadow gathering
to construct
collective memory
as
the sky burns.
posthumous
on the verge of promising.

A few months later, I pack up what little is mine and move into my own place.

There are cardboard boxes in the attic with my name on them. My mother insists I take them, so I do. I don't bother to look at what's inside.

My art table, folded, fits into the backseat of my car.

I've already made a mix-tape for this ride.

Mostly empty, the new space seems larger than when I first came to look it.

I notice: the entire apartment slants slightly to one side.

Sometimes in the middle of the living room, if I'm still long enough, I can feel the tilt, like a boat listing. The reclining lawn chair I trash-pick becomes a raft, the rescue kind.

My first job is with a medical publishing company. I am a page layout designer, medical textbooks. I prepare mechanical boards.

I slice galleys, each one flipside-coated in hot wax. I splice small typeset lines, subtract or add and shift even a single letter at a time.

I measure and make space for photographs and line art, position, crop, take originals to the Photostat camera—plug-in, crank-closed, flip, rotate, crank-open—to resize.

And my work in the darkroom with chemicals, those are whole other days.

It is physical, hands-on work. Repetitive.

A paycheck.

When I finally unpack the boxes stacked in my new kitchen, in one I find all my medals and ribbons and trophies. Beneath them, three of the Madame Alexander dolls from my childhood bedroom.

From inside the dolls, rubber bands dry-rotted. Plastic limbs detached.

Bodies, in pieces.

I imagine my mother's disappointment, recalling how concerned she had been for their well-being.

I do not remember choosing to keep any of these things, but here they are in the middle of my first apartment being repacked, taped closed, stored in a closet.

Some kept-things resist preservation.

Time loosens, unwinds.

I stop dreaming of the car accident itself, but the hospital room I'd once occupied continues to be a space I revisit in the ambiguity of sleep.

.　　　.　　　.

I inhabit the dream-space as endoskeleton—delicate glass, hand-spun.

Rolls of thin gauze and scarlet ribbon climb the walls.

A few weeks after I move into my apartment, I stop by to see my parents. When my father turns to say hello to me, I notice his face looks different somehow.

One side drooped, slightly.

"You alright, Dad?"

"I'm fine. Just running late."

I notice it even more when he speaks. His words slur.

The symmetry of his smile is off. Only one side of his mouth curls upward.

I convince him to come to the hospital with me.

And, right there, in pale-yellow pools of the same fluorescent light where I'd fought to stay alive after the accident—

right there, where they'd brought summer-fling-turned-love after the lightning strike—

right there, my father—

my father is crashing—

.   .   .

In a room siphoned of air, I take flight—

land in my childhood bed,

tuck myself in.

I sit beside my mother in a waiting room for hours. Just before sunrise, the neurosurgeon appears in the doorway, calls out my mother's name.

My mother's shoulders hunched forward, she grips my forearm, helps me to stand instead.

These are the exact words I write down as soon as the doctor walks away: Your father is not out of the woods—I removed a blood clot the size of a baseball—even so he suffered an ischemic stroke—Massive—We're keeping him completely sedated, in order to keep his intracranial pressure stable.

Any other words besides these seem far away, unreachable.

My mother sobs. Withers.

Time in this room expands and contracts, at once.

When I finally see my father post-surgery, I stand in the sliding-glass entrance, stare at him.

The room, a strange tableau.

His body, a tract of unfamiliar landforms.

Tubes sprout from the closed-up skin of his skull. Metal staples arc over the top like the tracks of a train.

I remember Christmas mornings, the train platform my father built: A piece of plywood. A tunnel dug from Styrofoam. Miniature houses and people. A Lionel train set. I picture his face, his smile widening as he presses the button to make the sound of the whistle.

Not long after I see him for that first time, my father is rushed back into surgery. Another clot, despite intervention. Another night stretching into morning. Another dialogue with the same neurosurgeon, more medical terms, a more dire prognosis.

Cerebral Vascular Accident (CVA)—An interruption in the flow of blood to cells in the brain—when cells in the brain are deprived of oxygen, they die.

Left-sided Hemiplegia—with damage to the right hemisphere of the brain—

A scan of my father's head shows more darkness than light.

Darkness collects me, as though I'm just another object, swept-up, piled into some sort of oblivion.

Some days, I can only watch as the warp and weft of a world goes on around (without) me. The warp of infrastructure, fixed, unfailing. The weft of everything drawn-through.

Swift. Exhausting.

I become preoccupied with my father's motionlessness.

I believe I see movement sometimes. The slightest flutter.

As I sit beside his bed, I tap on his forearm, keep pace with machine clicks and beeps, endless footfalls on the linoleum floor.

On quieter evenings, the sound of the clock ticking becomes a metronome, beats per minute. Sometimes I imagine song.

I speak often with my father's doctors. Sometimes a meeting is planned. Other times they just stop by. Uniformly calm. Their speech a monotone delivery of medical terms. And the occasional wonderment at my father's will to live.

I struggle with becoming my father's caregiver.

I am twenty-one.

Thirty days of stillness pass before my father's doctors decide it is safe—*though still risky*—to slowly wean him off the ventilator and bring him out of the drug-induced coma.

The days that follow feel turbulent. From bad to good, good to bad—hours, minutes, vacillate. Back and forth. Up and down.

My body, its emotions, its responses, swing like a gate, half-hinged. The force of repeated slams leaves me off-balance.

When my father is moved from ICU to a rehabilitation floor, the extent of his limitations magnify, seem unending.

I try to persuade my parents to see a counselor, join a stroke support group, anywhere they can go to talk about what's happened to their life. If it means they'll actually go, I offer to accompany them.

They refuse.

I imagine what looms.

If weathering is a process of disintegration, it had already been happening to their marriage—before his stroke.

And this, now, this is the slow process of erosion, large pieces shifting, washing away.

The breach of anything—everything—once shored-up.

And all I can do is watch. Up-close.

Later in the week, my father is moved to rehab.

I go. Every day. After work.

On my endless drives back and forth, between the rehab's location in the city and my apartment in the suburbs, I pass the sprawling tree-lined campus of Tyler School of Art. A friend has told me about a solo exhibit hanging in the gallery there and one day, spur of the moment, I finally stop.

Really, stop.

Kiki Smith. *Untitled.* 1990. Installation.

Floor-to-ceiling panels, handmade paper sheets on the walls of the gallery, are soaked, bloodred. From above, life-size paper bodies hang, dangling at the center of the room. Ghostlike.

And I think of my father. His body, frail now, deprived of firm footing. Everything that had once been his life, suspended.

Smith's bodies have been cast, paper left creased and textured like skin, emptied.

Weightless.

At first, the surrounding red walls seem separate from the bodies, each their own statement on fragility. Mortality.

But the more time I spend inside the space, the more connected they seem, as though the apparitional quality of the hanging [bodies] had been attained in part by leeching the blood from their veins.

I feel both inspired and overwhelmed. Note how, without words, Kiki Smith says everything about the body, disempowered.

A kind of transcendence found in surrender.

For a moment, my own body feels weightless, and I sense something beyond its physicality. Spirit-or-soul-like, perhaps. A profound feeling of connectedness. Though fleeting, as other thoughts intrude.

My father worsens emotionally and physically as he comes to realize the permanence of his condition.

Some days he refuses help in getting up out of bed. Some days he refuses physical therapy. Some days he becomes combative.

As he ignores his *affected* side, movement deteriorates, muscles atrophy.

His physical therapist calls it *learned nonuse*—it leads to a pattern of unilateral neglect. He effectively starts to act as though his left side does not even exist.

One night, I try to explain all of this to him.

"I've heard it all before," he says. "You're just repeating all the people who work here, using all their big words."

"I just want you to get as much help as you can while you're here, Dad. That's all. The people in PT want that for you, too."

"Well, who the hell said I wanted it?" He leans forward, rests his forehead in his right hand, frustrated, childlike.

I keep trying.

He squawks.

No living being can exist in isolation. What survives, what thrives, relies on the support of proximate organisms.

To root: To form, as a basis. To support.

Epiphytic roots enable a plant to grow on another plant, to acquire food and water from its host.

If symbiotic, the relationship will do no harm.

On the day he comes home from the rehab, at my father's request, I take a pair of scissors to his hair. In one hand I hold a fine-toothed comb, lift the strands of hair away from his scalp. With the other, I open the scissors, close them, twin-blades sliding past one another, metal grazing metal.

How a single silver screw allows the simultaneous gesture of the object's purpose and my intent.

When I finish cutting his hair, I trim the long wiry hairs of his eyebrows, reach the sharp silver tips into the moist caverns of his nose.

"You done yet?" he snaps.

"Almost. Stay still." I can hear the scolding in my voice.

I can see a boyishness in his eyes.

I begin dressing my father, starting with a long, white pair of socks. I roll them up in my hands then unroll them onto his feet. The occupational therapist had taught me each step I'd need to know.

He yells, suddenly, says I am hurting his toes. I slide the left leg into the pair of pants then follow with the right. I pull the zipper up.

He stares upward, his body a horizontal plane now, parallel to floor and ceiling.

I pull his shirt over his head, work to maneuver his left arm into the sleeve. Contracted and stiff, it clings tightly to his chest. I can't remember if I am doing this part in the right order.

I sense his frustration. With his right hand, he grabs his left arm, lifts it then lets it fall back hard against his body.

"It's useless," he spits. "Dead weight—just cut the whole fucking arm off."

.   .   .

I hear the sound of seams ripping,

imagined—   or not—

bolts of whipcord unwound, sheer-cut, bound

I have become the custodian of two halves of a body, both giving up—stiffening limbs on his left side and tired, weakening limbs on his right.

I have assigned myself this role, I suppose, in resigning to stay.

My mother, still, a shadow.

There. Not there.

At dinnertime, I stand back as she pushes my father's wheelchair to the dining room table for dinner. "Lift your feet. Use your good leg to lift the bad one," she yells, as his shoe catches on the carpet.

There is resentment in needing. There is resentment in being needed.

From the kitchen, she carries his plate, leaves it in front of him for a second before remembering she needs to cut the chicken into small pieces. I watch as she does this—each knife-slice louder, shriller, more exaggerated than the one before.

As she leans in toward him, I imagine barbed wire wrapped around both their upper bodies, binding them tightly, digging in, drawing blood.

Always, metal.

Always, a signature of sharps, arranging itself: F – C – G – D – A – E – B (remember: *Fast Cars Go Dangerously Around Every Bend*).

In the middle of a weekday afternoon, the phone call comes. My father pleads with me. “Please, just come help me up off the floor.”

I urge him to call 9-1-1. I offer to call for him. But he begs. “I’ll be fine. Just come help me.”

I find my father on his side, pinned between the bed and the wheelchair. I know there is no way I can lift him alone.

I dial 9-1-1, apologize to him and move the wheelchair just enough to lie down alongside him on the floor, eye to eye.

When I extend my hand toward his, he reaches out, squeezes my fingers.

He does not let go.

When two police officers arrive, I stand out of the way as they hoist my father up, onto a gurney.

His eyes widen, a look of fear I’d never seen before. “Thank you, young man, thank you,” he keeps saying, over and over. He grabs onto the sleeve of one of their jackets.

“You don’t have to worry, sir. We got you. We won’t let you fall.”

As I look at him later, squinting in the familiar fluorescence of the emergency room, my thoughts leap across a quarry.

Time cuts deep into rock, lets in light. And I see my father standing beside the shed he'd built years before, that place where he tinkered with things that smelled like gasoline and wet grass and wood. His t-shirt soaked with sweat. The lenses of his glasses darkened by the sun.

I want to stay here in this moment, to hear the sound of the shed door squeak open, to know that kind of certainty again.

Before her shift ends, the nurse brings news: Surgery will need to be scheduled to repair multiple fractures in my father's left hip.

I rest my hand on his shoulder. I do not let go.

A body, once inhabiting the wild, no longer free.

Tethered now to what reaches down, like the long tap roots of butterfly weed—deep—where darkness collects, where the earth closes in around everything held in place.

All the while, despite physical therapy appointments several times a week, my father's ability to move worsens. His limbs and tendons contract more, an Achilles contracture eventually taking him back into surgery.

His behavior becomes more erratic. Unpredictable.

His mental stability declining fast, and there is nothing I can do but note the steady rate at which this is happening.

Neither he nor my mother want to talk about professional support.

To consider any type of remedy is to admit vulnerability. To admit vulnerability is to accept accountability. To accept accountability is to trace the path that had brought them here to this point, to devote the time—the energy—to unraveling the byzantine tangle of fucked-up damage they'd both left long-untended.

I am tired.

In small increments, slowly, I attempt to distance myself.

How many times I have to let go, to turn away, so I will not break trying to fix my father. Trying to stand in for my mother.

How I'd heard her scream at him, in frustration, as she dressed him and bathed him. How I had watched the faint light in her extinguish.

Desperately, I want to show her compassion, to admit I understand.

But I, too, need care.

I think back to the butterflies, consider the necessary stages of their transformation. So sweeping, so complete in their spinning of a cocoon. Weeks passing, a body dormant, undergoing radical change.

Dissolving. Replacing.

Assembling. Differentiating.

In my mind, everything reduces to pattern.

Scale. Tiny pinpoints of light.

Spectral, lurking.

This place for me of juncture—past and present—life and death.

The body, ticking. Time, immobilized.

Eventually, my father is admitted to the behavioral health unit of a nearby hospital.

I dread visiting him there.

But my mother never goes.

The first time, I arrive to find him slumped forward in a green vinyl chair, wearing clothes that are not his own, the staff having dressed him in a stained shirt, pants both too wide in the waist and too short.

As I walk down the hallway toward him, I stop about five feet away from where he sits, swallow hard, try to stop myself from crying.

I lace my hands together, lift them toward my face. Prayer, perhaps.

A way to still myself for a second. Breathe.

"Are you his daughter?" one of the nurses asks.

It is a simple question, and I am almost certain I nod in response. But, at the same time, my heartbeat drums in my temples. My thoughts race.

I want to turn and run toward the red exit sign above the door.

No, I imagine myself saying, *he's not my father. This is all a mistake.*

"He's refusing to take his medication," one of the nurses says to me. "He thinks we're conspiring against him."

I know, in telling me this, they are expecting me to participate in some way.

And that expectation is like a speeding train headed straight for me.

Run. Run. Run. It's all I can think.

I take a deep breath, and another, and another. And another. Until finally I can lean in toward my father, cup my hand around his stubbly chin, lift his face enough to look into his eyes.

The man I once knew is not there.

I search desperately.

"Dad," my hand still supporting his head, "you need to take the medicine they're trying to give you. It's going to help."

I want to believe my own words.

"Please believe me. I'm here now, and I need you to start taking this medication." His eyes meet mine, fixed there long enough to see it is me, to hear what I say when twice more I repeat those same words.

Finally, he relents, lets me crush up the blue and pink and yellow pills, mix them into vanilla pudding.

I spoon the pudding into his mouth. Each time I raise the spoon to his lips, when his mouth opens, so does mine.

Before I leave, I kiss my father on the forehead. "For me. Take the medicine for me, so I know you're okay."

Once I get to my car, I lean my back up against the driver-side door, close my eyes, inhale. The air sweet now with spring flowers.

Daylight lengthening.

My father's psychiatrist calls me, rattles off a list of medications with impossible names I try to spell, write down.

I call and leave a message for the psychologist who'd administered tests a couple days before.

Days slide into each other, often, one indistinguishable from the next. My visits with my father in the behavioral unit of the hospital are brief.

Each time, I find him slumped forward, either in the green vinyl chair or in a wheelchair, parked in the hallway near the nurse's station.

Seeing him like this is unbearable.

First, his body as betrayal—now his mind.

When I speak to his psychologist, I write down the names of the tests he'd administered. A string of consonants and vowels: MMSE-WMS-BG-GDS.

Then, slowly, he delivers the results. I grip my pen.

poorly oriented—severe limitations in short & long-term memory—essential tremor in right hand at rest—noted more with movement—worsens considerably under stress—unable to write words or a complete sentence—social judgment exceptionally limited

I underline *exceptionally limited*, as the psychologist emphasizes it as he speaks. And, at the bottom of that page, inside a box, I write:

severe level of clinical depression—a complete collapse

My father is hospitalized. Sepsis, from a feeding tube insertion site.

This had, of course, been a risk, another in a constellation of risks.

He declines, fast.

His body, on fire, how it burns for hours without changing.

Through a window, two brown stink bugs crawl in, cling to a wall. I am fascinated by how they spend hours in the same place.

Diapause, a low-energy state caused by an inability to find food.

My own body, unmoving. My mind bundling tightly to the particulars of moments. Tangling.

Knotting, until I know I will never be able to separate the memory of my father's suffering from the strange stillness of two shield-shaped bugs on a hospital room wall.

I spend a stretch of days at his bedside.

A persistence. A duration.

[silence]

Outside, a flag snaps in the wind.

Rain falls sideways.

My father's eyes blink wide-open briefly.

Then close.

His chest rises.

Then falls.

I hold onto his right hand, his tremor gone now.

Mine worsening to a shudder.

The inevitability of genetics. Mendelian. Passed-down.

Carrying on.

Time now, a remembering. A want / need for forgiveness—all the kept things, released.

Perhaps the most impossible-looking thing

A half dozen or more— laid flat,

.   .   .

I dream my father

gliding along shorelines, setting down

wentletraps and whelks

and periwinkles for me to find.

Perfect Fibonacci spirals I fill my pockets with.

I will not recall much about the day of my father's funeral, except that I feel terribly alone.

My lungs water-logged.

Not long after, I make my way back to my childhood home, the place where I remember my father being happiest.

I find, of course, another family having long-built a life inside.

I knock, tell my story to the kind young mother who answers the door. Behind her, two toddler boys orbit the living room space. How much smaller it looks to me than it did when I was their age.

I ask her permission to stand at the gate, to look into the backyard.

My father's shed is gone. Nothing stands in its place.

Yet I photograph the yard anyway, capture what isn't there. Document a space from which everything I remember has been erased.

A red shed, a red picket fence. A father standing tall, beads of sweat on his face, eyes squinting in the sun.

.   .   .

Side-to-side, the weft—a single thread   pulled   through   memory—

how, when it's cut,

all things hushed

become affliction.

Not even two years pass, and I am faced again with the possibility of loss.

Its proximity.

In the months leading up to my mother's dying, time claims all the vibrant colors, brings cold.

Red and gold and orange slip away gradually. I notice it more than I ever had before.

Ivy vines turn the brown of tree trunks they'd spent the summer climbing. As winter grips my garden, everything breaks down.

Birds abandon backyard feeders. Chipmunks retreat into tunnels they'd burrowed into a crumbling stone wall.

My mother is disappearing, too. She coughs, wheezes. Her breath shallow, never enough air. Her chest tightens, in a way that alarms her, often.

pneumonia—emergency room visits—overnight hospital stays

Until finally she tells me she's had enough. "Don't let them take me to the hospital again. Don't let me linger."

She signs a do-not-hospitalize order. But I am certain, whenever the next crisis comes, she will want to disregard it. She'll want to live.

This, I believe.

But she does not. She does not waver at all.

Her fever spikes.

Her body shakes.

She is drowning, her lungs filling with fluid.

I want to read her poems, to play her favorite songs.

She wants silence.

"Don't let me linger." My mother asks for morphine, drains each dropper.

With her hand nested in mine, I stay motionless as her gasping breaths subside.
I rest my head on the bed's handrail, sob as her skin turns the color of sky.

Sibilants sharpen the blade of my tongue, push past, make a hissing sound.

In the days that follow, I spend hours leafing through notebooks I discover among my mother's things. Marbled composition books I'd never seen before, filled with flowery love poems.

So much longing. Perhaps a want for something she had never known in this life.

At my desk, I type up the first twenty or thirty pages of her poems. At first, I do this to see what it is to spend time inside her head, her thoughts, to experience the kind of feelings, deep and insightful, she never shared with anyone, or at least not with me.

I print those typed-up poems.

I stare at them for a while then take white acrylic paint and a brush to each page.

I don't want to alter the notebooks themselves—a need I have to preserve the perfect loops and curls of her Catholic-school penmanship.

Instead, I white-out words on the pages I've typed.

Erasure is a form of poetry created by taking away words from an existing text.

because
I
believed
beyond
feeling
must be
happiness,

I went
alone,
miles,
declared
you

shadow memory.
The sound that is your voice
every word

the echo
of
what is hidden in your heart, again
and again

you turn into

the empty space

the dark blue hollow

You are
a thousand notes

without sound
wishful thinking

I have put away
:
doubt
that lingers
did you
ever see
me?

Erasure is an act of reframing.

A series of marks left. A space opened for light.

For me, now, an affirmation: *Here she was, this woman, my mother.*

I am in the middle of writing my MFA thesis (about my mother) when my mother dies.

I stop writing. Every word too sharp. Every word, a betrayal.

Language, far-off. The page, a distant other-planet.

Weeks pass.

Finally, the empathy of a writing mentor comforts me, a kind of mercy that gently leads me back to the page.

But what I write is wordy, composed without attention to cadence or sound.

What I write is dense, pages of prose that make little use of white space.

What I write relies solely on narrative voice.

Somewhere, amidst a succession of losses, I lose myself.

Without reason, I put away my art to focus on my writing. Pack it up neatly, set it aside, as though it never happened at all. A necessary sacrifice—or so I think—if I want to be taken seriously as a writer.

For me, there exists no space for both.

Until, in a poetry class, I am introduced to ekphrasis—a verbal description of a visual work of art—where I find that middle place, where facts, reflections, and feelings intersect—merge, mingle, stir-up—at the confluence of the visual and the verbal.

Where what sets them apart dissolves. Where boundaries break down and form becomes expandable, accommodating. Speculative, pliant.

Sometimes, for me, this literary device is expressed in the form of a conversation. Or an imagined story. Sometimes, it is the catalyst for research. Or it becomes a useful tool in revision.

A layering up of context, meaning.

How I discover the unbounded possibility that exists between what is observed and what can be expressed. How I come to know the difference, too, between what I see and what I want others to see.

My own body as installation: mixed-media construction: salvage alongside ruin.

The materials vary: Spools of thread. Plaster. Layers of gauze, tangles of tape. Crumpled paper gowns.

Ink, too, and seven tiny bug pins* positioned close together in a tattoo gun. The force of puncture through layers of skin.

Cells steeped in pigment. Body as canvas *and* as story-told, made permanent.

A monarch butterfly on my forearm first, then a tiger swallowtail.

Tattoo as atonement. Redemption.

> A thing of reflection. Humility.
>
> A thing of release. Liberation.

How I keep trying to forgive myself.

---

* The same pins used by entomologists to mount insects for display.
* The same pins used by me & my father to pin butterflies years ago.

For too long, in every story I conjure, in every tale I tell, I am the victim.
My thoughts manifest, startlingly physical in their weight, their unwieldiness.
I carry them everywhere, along a continuum of dread.

This is how I exist in the world, though I keep trying to write a very different story. Revision after revision. And I seek out women artists to whom I can look for inspiration, as I slowly build my own creative life. A daily practice.

In Frida Kahlo, I come to know a teacher, a woman who had known the sudden devastation of an accident as I did.

Hers was a body pulled almost gravitationally toward injury, and yet her paintings point ceaselessly at grace.

I am transfixed first by her plaster corsets, how she hand-painted each one, turned clinical objects—rigid enclosures imprisoning her body—
into evocative and haunting extensions of herself. Meditations on the power of creativity to sustain and heal the mind and body, to face unbounded loss, to confront unbearable longing.

From Frida, I begin learning how to translate this body I inhabit.

New York City becomes for me a frequent destination. A train ride. An escape. Where I go sometimes on weekends to wander the vast rooms of museums.

It is strange to note how small I feel there physically yet at once how my mind expands, fills with ideas.

The intensity of experience, the clarity.

One weekend, at the Whitney Museum, I find Kiki Smith again, a much more expansive exhibit of her work this time.

It feels both familiar and disorienting.

What I see first is *Untitled*, like much of her work. An installation of twelve glass water bottles that resemble antique medical specimen jars. Each bottle is empty and etched in Gothic lettering with the name of a bodily fluid, from life-sustaining (blood, semen, milk) to disease-bearing (pus, vomit).

I've never seen anything quite like this, and I cannot move away from it. Perhaps it's curiosity that keeps me there, perhaps disgust. Maybe both.

What I do know for sure is the obsession that follows.

The awe and respect.

As I wander through the exhibit, I marvel at how her work can be at once beautiful and alluring, vile and revolting. Dizzied, I lose myself in the shifting trajectory of each nonnarrative, nonlinear story.

There exists a razor-sharpness. A devastation.

The way her process—her imagination, her manipulation of materials—leads me to reconsider, to challenge, every convention I've held about the making of art.

In the museum shop, I buy my first art book: *Kiki Smith: A Gathering, 1980-2005.* I page through from cover to cover on the train ride back home.

I take it all in, and I learn. But I want—need—to find my own voice.
I cannot imagine what it will sound like, how it might make itself heard.

.   .   .

Imagine a language shaped

by revelation,

by sharp angles of light.

Imagine a new city, the new start it promises.

To move, not only in the sense of miles-in-between, but in the way of mercy.

I learn this slowly.

Preservation instinct: Making deliberate choices. Building a stable life.

Hundreds of therapy hours logged, time devoted to emotionally dismantling the house of silence I'd spent years constructing / dwelling inside.

To move: Away-from. Toward. Maps drawn to trace the difference.

A new city, the new start it promises.

Not the long-sullied place I'd called home. Not the hustle of Manhattan. But a smaller city of bridges, their passage, their bright-yellow promise welcoming us.

Me. My husband. Our two dogs. Trying to imagine the shape of some other life. Less ruffled.

More restful.

A place to keep mending. To believe it possible.

Then.

On an ordinary weekday.

In the early afternoon.

On a busy road.

In a matter of seconds.

How it all comes undone: the work of healing.

How it all returns: the rattle, the irrefutable fact that nowhere is safe.

And the red of stained glass church windows. And the red of roses being peddled by a man on the side of the road.

A car stopped ahead. A traffic light, the red of remembering.

From behind, the blare of a horn, the screech of tires. The unexpected force of impact, a body flung forward.

My body.

Again.

The red of blood, its trickle along my temple.

My husband beside me, makes sure I am conscious, then pries his emergency kit from the smashed-in trunk. Disappears.

Much later, after the scans of my head and the stitching of my skin, he will tell me the dismal story of the overdosed driver, how he hauled the heft of his lifeless body from the wreck of the car out onto the street, his face bearded and bloody and turned the blue of carapace, of lesser crab.

And how he breathed for him through a mask until an ambulance arrived and EMTs shot Narcan into his shoulder and he started to cough and, by the time my husband reaches this point in his account, I realize I have been holding my breath, knowing everything unlearned—all the fear-thirsty, anxiety-fed thoughts—were returning fast.

Louder and louder.

Unrelenting.

How this tunnels deep, cellularly.

How the body's immune system responds to recurring exposure to stressors, to the persistent triggers of trauma. Its aftermath.

On the skin above my ankles first, a bright-red pattern appears, profuse. Unexpected.

Alarming, as it climbs, clings to tender skin covering the trellised vertebrae of my spine.

Red trumpet vine.

This, the start of a bloom, my back a botanical garden—inked already with flowers, a butterfly.

My body as collective noun:

> A field of poppies.
>
> A plume.
>
> An inflorescence.
>
> A tangle of bittersweet,
> spindle, chokeberry.
>
> A throng of invasive threats.

Layers of cells keep stacking one on top of another—flat scales, inflamed-red.

A proliferation. Strata, in a dis-ordered system.

My body, its misfires. Flare after flare.

.   .   .

Butterflies alight in the nest of my hair.

I invite them to stay.

I am fragile, too, I confess,   stilled now mid-flight.

My body as unbearable.

In the mirror, I stare at an abundance of red circles on my skin. Stippled. Everywhere.

In the mirror, I glimpse the memory of a girl, nineteen, the red scars. Crosshatched. Everywhere.

And I want to save her.

Then.

Now.

From breaking.

From being emptied.

.   .   .

I go to places of harm,

hands pressed

to a cold tile floor.

What befalls, builds up.

Autoimmune (predisposed). Self-destruction (prone to).

Under normal circumstances, inflammation in the body starts when a T-cell detects a disease-causing pathogen somewhere in the body.

Skin flares like mine happen in the absence of a pathogen. T-cells, without reason, suddenly migrate to the skin's outer layer, secreting tumor necrosis factor (TNF) as if the body is under attack.

Skin cells hyperproduce. Where it usually takes twenty-eight to thirty days for these cells to form and shed, that time is reduced, happening instead within three to five days, cells pushing through my body's protective outer layer.

Skin layering up, constricting, causing pain. The firing of sensory neurons, transmitting electrical impulses to the spinal cord, then to the brain.

For weeks, undiagnosed, I tell myself stories, the terrible sort.

As I wander hallways of a hospital, the past and all its sterile rooms swerve back toward me.

Everything the same, in its immensity.

Everything fluorescent, aflame.

One study, one test, after another.

Again, my body, a proving ground.

And I find myself back inside that circle, the one drawn as limitation, as *everything-bad-that-happened-to-me.*

In moments of stillness, though, in waiting rooms and exam rooms, I let myself imagine the artist I want to be, dream of how my art might save me.

I begin to collage and paint, build up texture, tentatively. I sand and scratch, peel away and cut out and overlay.

In each project, its process, I am drawn to both the force of destruction and the beauty of transformation.

Within that paradox, I reside.

. . .

On the worst days,

I talk to Frida about desire.

I spend months exhausted—by the autoimmune disease and by its cure—methotrexate, a chemo drug I swallow every seven days, a drug that, according to my insurance company, must *fail first* before my doctor can prescribe the biologic I need.

Fail.

Students fail. Hearts fail. Banks fail.

Most often, there's a rubric or a tracker or a series of documents by which to measure such an assessment.

By what metric can methotrexate's failure be measured? By whom?

I am the only one who can say whether it is or isn't working. I am the only one inhabiting this skin, its flares worsening, becoming more frequent.

My body, a house on fire.

I am almost always nauseous from the drug. And, in the cruelest irony, alone, I spend hours heaving on the bathroom floor.

I attempt to document, to diagram the profusion of my body's flare at its worst.

What results, more a pointillist drawing.

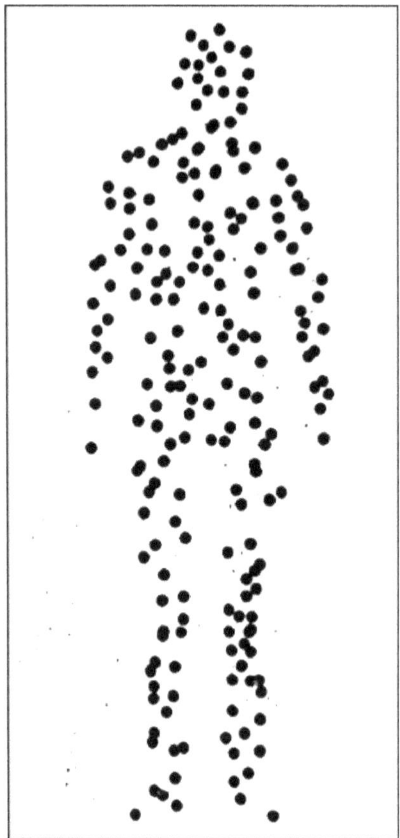

A connect-the-dots.

Inside, all summer long, I swallow the poison.

Wait.

Swallow the poison.

Wait.

Outside, blight.

Leaf spot pathogens climb aspens and poplars, cankers girdling stems.
Rust disease infects rose bushes, hawthorn trees.

Galls form like blisters on leaves of the neighborhood's largest white oak.

On my balcony, aphids spread, feast on every plant.

Everywhere, spotted lantern flies swarm.

A plague. Biblical.

Tens of thousands fall from the sky, from treetops and telephone poles, cover sidewalks and streets. Red wings flutter—land—leap—sputter—too often, escape. The movement of my feet, a maniacal dance. Reach around, stomp. Piqué arabesque, grand plié. A choreography of madness.

Despair.

When the medication I need is approved, finally, a nurse ambassador from the drug company calls to guide me through what I learn will be a lifetime of self-administered injections.

She says: *The thigh is best. Or the stomach.*

She sends a tutorial video.

She says: *There is no cure.*

She suggests I keep a journal. To track progress. To record triggers, if breakthrough flares occur. To be an active participant in my care.

On the first page, I write: *Fuck this. And fuck resilience. I am tired of fighting.*

I search for light from somewhere deep inside a persistent darkness.

Slowly, art-making returns to me. I struggle with the way it feels at first. Unfamiliar. Laborious. But I find an opening, eventually, access to an entire other world, one I disappear into. Often.

Mixed media. Photography. Illustration. Collage. I begin to see everything in terms of composition—each mark made, each piece placed, with intention.

Part research project, part devotional act.

I study Frida's vocabulary of color: *Gold was sunlight on asphalt. Gold was the gleam of metal through an open wound. Magenta, on the other hand, was the color of blood.*

Again and again, the word process insists I consider its place in all of this.

Process, as in a series of steps taken.

Progression.

Process, as in practice, discipline.

Further study.

How I chronicle each attempt at making, each material's response. Detailed notes kept in a sketchbook—focus on method, means, rather than object-made.

And, as I settle into this rhythm of sustained practice, I begin to feel my body loosen.

Let go.

Though, still, I feel its resistance sometimes, as if to say, *it hurts being reborn.*

Other Voices

Page 16:
Centers for Disease Control and Prevention
https://www.cdc.gov/nceh/hearing_loss/what_noises_cause_hearing_loss

Page 22:
"Misophonia is associated with altered brain activity in the auditory cortex and salience network," *Scientific Reports,* Volume 9, Article number: 7542, 2019

Page 68:
National Institute of Mental Health
https://www.nimh.nih.gov/health/topics/post-traumatic-stress-disorder-ptsd

Page 83:
found text from 1988 newspaper clippings

Page 98:
Kiki Smith: A Gathering, 1980-2005, Linda Lochlin, 33

Page 101:
3.2.4: *Root Modifications,* Melissa Ha, Maria Morrow, and Kammy Algiers, Yuba College, College of the Redwoods, & Ventura College via ASCCC Open Educational Resources Initiative

Page 117:
Schlitz Audubon Nature Center
https://www.schlitzaudubon.org/2020/11/16/how-insects-survive-the-winter-diapause/

Page 134:
"Frida's Corsets," Leslie Jamison, *The Paris Review*, August 2011

Page 135:
Kiki Smith: A Gathering, 1980-2005, Marina Warner, 44, 52

Page 146:
National Library of Medicine
https://www.ncbi.nlm.nih.gov/pmc/articles/PMC7962638/

Page 155:
"Frida's Corsets," Leslie Jamison, *The Paris Review,* August 2011

Acknowledgements

Many thanks to the editors of the following publications, where excerpts of this book first appeared, sometimes in a slightly different form: Crab Creek Review, Lumina, Philadelphia Stories, terrain.org, Sonora Review.

And many thanks to my graduate school mentors at the Rainier Writing Workshop, where this book first began as my MFA thesis. Brenda Miller, Rebecca McClanahan, Marjorie Sandor, and Judith Kitchen—I will never forget what I learned from each of you. And I am forever grateful for the patience and guidance you gave me as I navigated the death of both of my parents during that time.

Thank you to friends for your feedback and ongoing support of my work on this book, as its making spanned many years: Natalie Tilghman, Liz Shine, Autumn Konopka, Chelsey Clammer, Cam Finch, Christopher Eckman, Jane Graille, Christi Wilcox. And much, much gratitude to Maralynn Jacoby, for your brilliant creativity and cover design.

Thank you to Jessica Gigot for choosing my manuscript in Minerva Rising's 2023 Memoir Contest and to Kim Brown for every single suggestion and edit that made this book even better as we went through the editing process. And I am so grateful to Brooke Schultz, Minerva Rising's graphic designer, who made every single page perfect.

Most of all, thank you to my husband, Steve, for believing in me and supporting me through this journey. Ours is a whole other story—fate certainly had some crazy plans for us, all those years ago. I love you.

Kristina Moriconi is a writer and visual artist whose work has appeared in a variety of journals and magazines including *After the Art, terrain, About Place, Assembla* and *Photo Trouvée.* Her lyric narrative In the Cloakroom of Proper Musings was published by Atmosphere Press in August 2020. She lives in the woods outside Pittsburgh with her husband and three dogs.

www.ingramcontent.com/pod-product-compliance
Lightning Source LLC
LaVergne TN
LVHW060623110826
845147LV00015B/920

* 9 7 8 1 9 5 0 8 1 1 2 5 0 *